Microsoft Outlook Guide to Success:

Learn in a Guided Way to Create, Manage & Organize Your E-mails to Optimize Your Tasks & Surprise Your Bosses And Colleagues | Big Four Consulting Firms Method

Copyright © 2022
Kevin Pitch

TABLE OF CONTENTS

INTRODUCTION 3

1   SOFTWARE INTERFACE AND USE.................................9

2   CONTACTS 18

3   E-MAIL ORGANIZATION...20

4   CALENDAR...23

5   SECURITY...29

6   THE BEST OUTLOOK APPS/PLUGINS........................31

7   TIPS, TRICKS & FAQ WITH COMMON PROBLEMS AND SOLUTIONS...37

8   ADMINISTRATOR OUTLOOK....................................43

9   THE STRATEGIC SHORTCUTS....................................44

10   CONCLUSION..45

INTRODUCTION

The Microsoft Office suite includes a personal information manager called Microsoft Outlook.

What is Microsoft Outlook?

It is primarily an e-mail client but can also be used for web browsing, note-taking, contact management and task. It also has various other features, including the ability to create and edit a calendar.

You'll find a list of all your Outlook accounts in the Personal Folders File section of the Outlook window. Each of these accounts has its folder, and messages are stored there. In addition, you can see a preview of your e-mails in the To-Do bar or your Tasks, or you can see them on your calendar. You can also find different e-mail options through Quick Parts, which are like organized galleries. These features make it easy to organize your workspace and manage your e-mails.

Microsoft Outlook is a proprietary email client with built-in calendar, contact, and task management, as well as industry-leading support for Internet standards-based messaging platforms. Microsoft Office, Microsoft Exchange Server, and Internet Explorer are also integrated. This ensures that all your Microsoft applications work well together, and you won't have to worry about mismatches between applications. Plus, the Outlook interface is consistent across all platforms so that you can see all your information in one place.

Microsoft Outlook is available for Windows, Mac, mobile phones, and the web. You download the software from the Microsoft website and follow the installation instructions. The installation wizard will guide you through setting up the software. You can also get an Outlook CD-ROM if you want to install Outlook offline.

Where to buy or download

Microsoft Outlook is an e-mail application that can be downloaded and installed on computers. It is compatible with Mac and Windows computers and can also be used for webmail. This e-mail application has an integrated calendar, contact management features, and an address book. It syncs with other devices and includes a virtual sticky note tool for storing notes. It can also be downloaded on Android and iOS devices. It can also be integrated with many business applications.

You can buy Microsoft Outlook as a standalone application or download it from the Microsoft website. After downloading the application, follow the prompts to install it. A wizard will walk you through the installation process. You can download Outlook to your computer using a CD-ROM if you don't have an Internet connection.

Microsoft Outlook is a highly-rated e-mail client. It comes with excellent features and is easy to use. It also offers easy-to-read message previews, a side-by-side calendar, and other features. In addition, it's a secure application that won't sell or share your personal information with advertisers.

It's also a popular choice for professionals. Many businesses use Outlook, which easily manages calendars, to-do lists, and contacts. Outlook is also part of Microsoft's 365 suite of productivity applications. If you aren't sure whether Microsoft Outlook is right for you, try out the free 30-day trial before making a decision.

Where to use Microsoft Outlook?

Microsoft Outlook has many useful features for managing your e-mail. Its calendar feature helps you track meetings, appointments, and work tasks. Outlook can also help you organize your to-do list. It can also help you send e-mail appointment requests and meeting invitations. Outlook does all of these functions without requiring you to open separate applications. You can use Outlook's calendar to view events for the whole day or up to five days.

Microsoft's support center has a vast knowledge base that contains helpful articles about all Microsoft products, including Outlook. In addition, you can also find videos and walkthroughs on how to use Outlook on Windows 10, Mac, mobile devices, and the web. These resources are free to download and can be found by searching for Outlook on any device.

Outlook is a powerful e-mail application that is part of the Microsoft Office suite. It can be used on your personal computer or a business network. It offers an e-mail calendar, contacts, and task management and is part of Microsoft Office 365. You can also use it on mobile devices like Windows phones and tablets. Using Microsoft Outlook in a business environment, you'll find many ways to collaborate with co-workers and customers.

One of the most important things when using Outlook is organizing your e-mails. A cluttered inbox can make it hard to find essential e-mails, so an intuitive folder system can help you organize your e-mails easily. This will save you hours of searching for e-mails. You can also use Outlook's e-mail templates, which make it easy to send and receive e-mails.

Microsoft Outlook Vs. Other Applications

Microsoft Outlook is the premium e-mail application that comes as part of Microsoft Office. Despite its high price tag, Microsoft has improved Outlook over the years and has been designed to increase productivity. Windows Mail is fine for daily e-mail check-ups, but if you want to check your e-mail more often, Outlook is the way to go.

Microsoft Outlook vs. Gmail

Microsoft Outlook has long been the king of business e-mail solutions, but Google has revamped the industry with innovative services. While Office has been a desktop-centric software suite, G Suite is designed for the cloud. As a result, both programs can respond to customer feedback faster and roll out new features more quickly.

While apps take over real-time communication, e-mails are still king in business. However, if you use both, it is essential to know the pros and cons of each. So let's look at the pros and cons of Outlook and Gmail. Which one is right for you?

Both e-mail services have different features and layouts. Gmail's interface is cleaner and more intuitive, while Outlook's is more customizable. While Gmail is free for individuals, working professionals may require a paid account. Outlook's interface is instantly familiar to those familiar with Microsoft Office. Both e-mail programs offer built-in spam detection.

Gmail has more features, including advanced search. For example, Gmail allows you to search for messages based on their categories. Microsoft Outlook lets you carpet messages with different colors, but Gmail enables you to mark important messages with stars. You can also apply descriptive tags to messages. This feature allows you to follow up more thoroughly on client conversations.

Outlook offers a more traditional file system for e-mail organization and is easier to use for new users. Gmail relies on labels to organize e-mail messages, but users must create labels for each. As a result, Gmail's feature can benefit some people, but it cannot be very clear for others.

Microsoft Outlook vs. Apple Mail

Microsoft Outlook is one of the leading e-mail clients available for Mac users, but Apple Mail is free and comes with the Mac operating system. Both e-mail clients offer the same functionality, but Apple Mail has unique features and is much easier to use. For instance, it allows you to set VIPs, which means you will get priority mail from them. Moreover, the Apple Mail interface is simple and intuitive, so beginners will likely prefer it.

Apple Mail can only be used in the Apple ecosystem. Unlike Outlook, Apple Mail is only available for macOS, iPhone, and iPad users. Because of its Apple-only nature, it's not universally compatible with other operating systems. On the other hand, Outlook can be used on Mac OS, Windows, and Android. This makes it an excellent choice for Mac users.

Outlook offers more features and is more stable and secure. Compared to Apple Mail, it is more streamlined and easy to use. It is also available as part of Office 365, with several other features that make it a more professional application. Both are good choices for business users, and users may want to decide based on their individual needs.

Both Apple and Microsoft mail have their advantages. Apple mail has many features that Mac users can't get on an iPhone or iPad, but the user interface is similar, which makes it easier to use. However, Outlook is more complex than Apple Mail and uses more CPU resources. However, it offers many features, including a calendar, task list, and to-do list.

Microsoft Outlook vs. Thunderbird

Microsoft Outlook and Thunderbird are two of the most widely used desktop email programs. Both have a wide range of features and have different strengths and weaknesses. Thunderbird has an easy-to-use interface, while Outlook has a more robust feature set. Microsoft Outlook is the better choice for businesses since it has a better link to Microsoft Exchange servers.

Thunderbird is an excellent choice if you use several e-mail accounts. It allows you to manage an unlimited number of e-mail accounts without switching between multiple e-mail programs. It also features a unifying view, which is convenient when managing multiple accounts. However, Thunderbird has some limitations, and you may have to reset the application after installing add-ons.

Thunderbird is an open-source e-mail client that can be downloaded for free. In contrast, Microsoft Outlook requires a subscription to Microsoft Office. Thunderbird is available for various platforms, including Linux and Mac OS X. The Thunderbird Foundation continues to develop the e-mail client. This allows it to be accessible on more computers than Microsoft Outlook.

Microsoft Outlook has many advanced features, such as spam filters and firewalls. However, Thunderbird is a free, cross-platform e-mail application. So regardless of the operating system, Thunderbird can make life easier for businesses.

1 SOFTWARE INTERFACE AND USE

The Microsoft Office suite includes a personal information manager called Microsoft Outlook. The application is most commonly used as an e-mail client but includes other features such as calendaring, contact management, task management, and web browsing. Learn how to organize and manage your e-mails and other important information using these features.

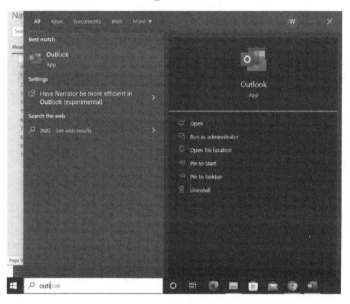

Figure 1: Accessing MS Outlook from Start Menu

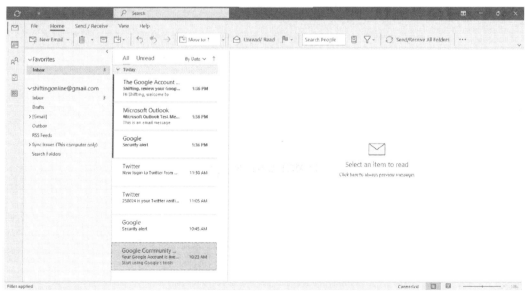

Figure 2: The Outlook Platform

1.1 What is cc in Microsoft Outlook?

CC stands for carbon copy, whereas BCC stands for blind carbon copy. This allows you to send one e-mail to multiple recipients and hides their e-mail addresses. CC is used when you want to send a copy of the message to more than one recipient, but BCC is used when you want to send the message only to certain people

The Cc field is used when you want to send an e-mail to someone else but does not want the recipient to read it. For example, when sending an e-mail, you can add as many people as you like in the To field. However, you don't want to add so many people to your e-mail that it makes your recipients feel like they must do something. By using Cc, you can ensure that all recipients receive your e-mail. Additionally, it enables you to send courtesy copies to parties with whom you may not be in direct communication.

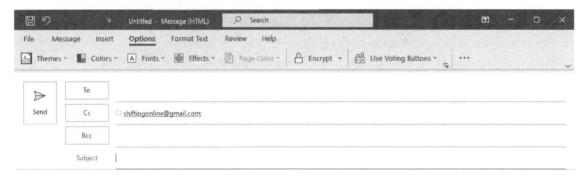

Figure 3: The CC and Bcc features

While CC and BCC are often debated, they are similar in their functionality. BCC stands for "blind carbon copy." When you send an e-mail to your manager, you can specify BCC to send a copy to the manager, for example. The CC and BCC fields will automatically appear each time you send an e-mail message.

The Cc field can also help protect your privacy. The Bcc recipient cannot see your replies unless they are on the Bcc line. However, you should remember that BCC recipients are often spammers. For this reason, most e-mail service providers limit the number of people they allow on BCC. Therefore, it is best to ensure the people you want to send e-mails to are on your safe sender list.

1.2 What is ccn in Microsoft Outlook?

Ccn is a common feature in Microsoft Outlook that allows you to send a message to a selected group of recipients. Using this feature is useful when you need to send a message to many partners with different addresses. In addition, this feature protects your contact information from being sent to the wrong people.

Adding a new contact group in Microsoft Outlook is simple. First, open Outlook. Then click on the "Add Group" tab. Next, click the "+" sign next to the group you wish to add. You will then be given a list of the groups available to you. Once you've added your groups, you can remove the duplicates.

You can also automatically include BCC recipients in your e-mails by installing the Compliance Copies add-in. This add-in works similarly to the Always BCC feature. However, it uses a more complicated set of rules to determine who to BCC. You can also set exceptions for this feature.

Another new feature is called @mentions. This feature will help you manage tasks and e-mails with more ease. For example, you can click the @mentions button in the reading pane to let the sender know that you liked the e-mail. This can be particularly useful if you have an e-mail from your manager saying you've done a great job on your TPS reports. Instead of typing "thanks," you can press the "+" button to let your manager know how much you appreciate their feedback.

1.3 What is reply to all in Microsoft Outlook?

You can use the reply All feature when you reply to multiple people. This will enable you to include all recipients' e-mail addresses in your reply. However, it is essential to note that Outlook does not automatically include the address that sent the message in the reply. It assumes that the sender has access to the original attachments. If this is an issue, there are workarounds.

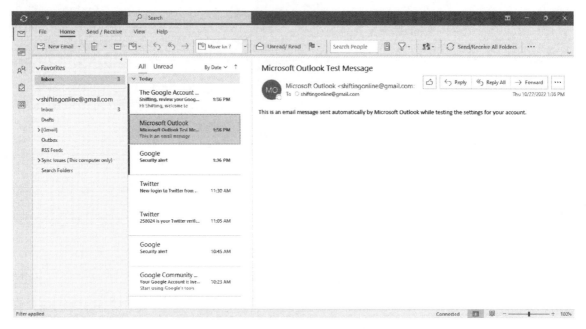

Figure 4: The Reply All feature

If you want to prevent the feature from being used by others, you can disable the "reply to all" feature. You can do this through the Developer tab on the ribbon. In the Developer tab, select "Design a form." Then, select "Reply to All." In the Properties window, uncheck "Enabled" and click "OK."

Reply to all has caused plenty of drama in offices. According to the VoloMetrix email-timing company, office workers spend as much as 15 percent of their time replying to e-mails. And about 5 percent of those e-mails contain "reply-all" messages. That's a staggering amount of time, costing a company tens of millions of dollars every year.

While reply-all users have been abusing the feature, servers are now better able to handle the traffic. This change was made to combat this behavior. However, users still abuse reply-all to a large extent. This problem has plagued Microsoft for years.

1.4 Creating a signature

Outlook.com allows you to create only one signature, which you can include when you want. For instance, you might use a very grand and formal signature for business to impress lackeys and sycophants and intimidate enemies. Unless, of course, you only have lackeys and sycophants as friends, in which case you should leave it off your messages. You certainly should go heavy on the praise, Your Royal Highness!

Following these steps will allow you to add a signature to Outlook.com:

- At the top of Outlook.com Mail, click the Settings icon.

- Click View Full Settings at the bottom of the pane.

- A dialog box appears.

- Select Compose and Reply from the middle pane.

- A box appears for the signature.

- Fill in the signature field with your text.

- Format your text as desired using the tools above the box.

- You can now click "Save."

The Settings dialog box is closed.

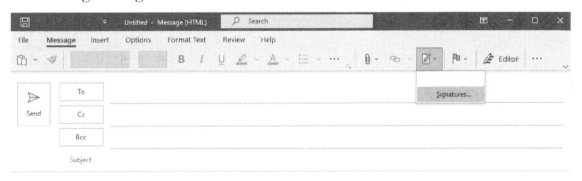

Figure 5: Signatures

How to Include E-mail Signatures

Make your signatures to add to your e-mails' bottom lines. Text, pictures, a symbol, an online commercial card, and even a picture of your scribbled signature are all acceptable forms of a signature. To create a signature, follow the steps below:

1. Select signature> Signatures in a new e-mail.

2. Select New from the E-mail Signature section.

3. Enter a username, then hit OK.

4. Do the following under Choose default signature:

   - Select an e-mail account linked to the signature from the list of available accounts.

   - Select the signature you wish to permanently apply to every new e-mail response from the list of new messages. You can disregard this option if you don't wish to automatically sign your e-mail letters because (none) is the default selection.

   - Select the signature you wish to be automatically inserted (auto-signed) when you respond to or forward e-mails from the Replies/forwards box. Alternatively, choose the default choice of (none).

5. Enter the signature beneath the Edit signature, after which hit OK.

6. Select the signature in a brief message, then pick the desired signature.

To add a command from the ribbon to the Quick Access Toolbar

1. Choose one of the following options:

   - Right-click a ribbon command and choose to **Add to Quick Access Toolbar**. You may add any command, including a drop-down menu of selections or a thumbnail gallery.

   - Click the **Customize Quick Access Toolbar button** at the right end of the Quick Access Toolbar. Next, select a command to add from the selection of frequently used commands.

To open the Outlook Options dialog box's Quick Access Toolbar page

1. Complete one of the following tasks:

   - Click the **Customize Quick Access Toolbar button** at the right end of the Quick Access Toolbar, then **More Commands**.

   - Select the **File tab**, then select **Options** in the Backstage view's left pane. **Next, click Quick Access Toolbar** in the left pane of the Outlook Options dialog box.

   - Right-click any ribbon tab or space, then choose Customize Quick Access Toolbar from the context menu.

From the Outlook Options dialog box, add a command to the Quick Access Toolbar

1. Open the Outlook Options dialog box and the Quick Access Toolbar page.

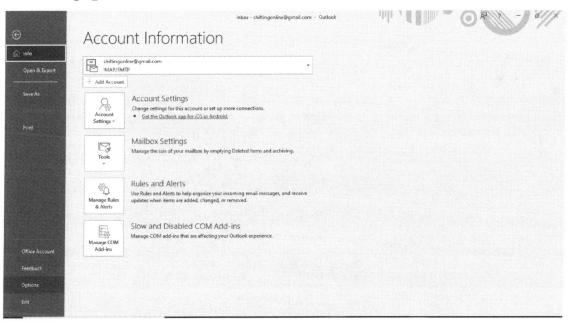

Figure 6: Heading to the Outlook Options

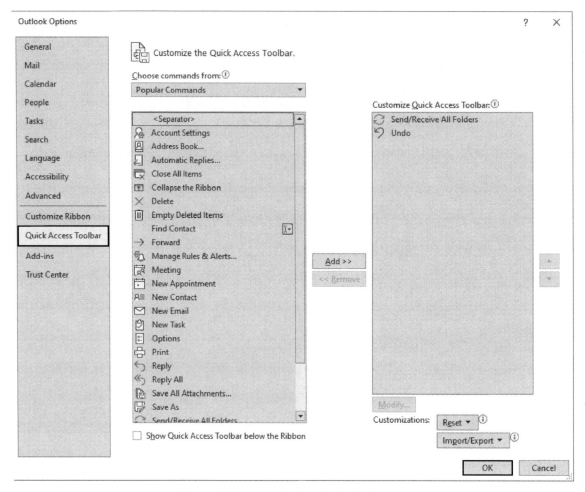

Figure 7: Features Under Outlook Options

2. Pick the tab the command appears on in the Choose commands from list, or click **Popular Commands, Commands Not on the Ribbon, All Commands, or Macros**.

3. Locate and click the command you wish to add to the Quick Access Toolbar in the Choose **commands from the window**. After that, press the **Add button**.

Display a divider on Quick Access Toolbar

1. Open the Outlook Options dialog box and the Quick Access Toolbar page.

2. Click the command you wish to enter the separator after in the right pane.

3. Choose one of the following options:

- Double-click Separator> on the left pane.
- In the left pane, choose separator, then click the **Add button**.

To move the Quick Access Toolbar's buttons

1. Open the Outlook Options dialog box and the Quick Access Toolbar page.

2. Click the button you wish to move in the right pane. Then, drag the button to the desired location using the Move Up or Move Down arrows.

To relocate the Quick Access Toolbar

1. Choose one of the following options:

- Click the **Customize Quick Access Toolbar button** at the right end of the Quick Access Toolbar, then Show Below the Ribbon or Show Above the Ribbon.

- Open the Outlook Options dialog box and the Quick Access Toolbar page. Next, select or clear the Show Quick Access Toolbar below the Ribbon check box in the space below the Choose **commands** from the list check box.

How to restore the Quick Access Toolbar

1. Open the Outlook Options dialog box and the Quick Access Toolbar page.

2. **Click Reset** in the lower-right corner, then choose one of the following options:

- Only the Quick Access Toolbar should be reset.

- Clear all personalizations.

3. **Click Yes** in the Microsoft Office dialog box that confirms the modification.

2 CONTACTS

People are the collective noun for the individuals and organizations that make up your professional and social networks. The only constraints that could apply to who you could or cannot add as a contact are those you or your employer impose. Whoever you include as a contact is entirely at your discretion. For instance, your organization may have policies regarding communication with particular external e-mail accounts.

2.1 How to create a contact

Contact may be as straightforward as a username and an e-mail account, or you could include more information, such as physical addresses, numerous telephone numbers, a photo, and anniversaries. Your contacts are located in the People section of the favorites menu in the Outlook window's lower left-hand corner. Go to People and select New Contact. You can also use Ctrl+Shift+C to establish contact from any folder.

Get a list of the contacts in your Outlook address book

It's a good idea to have a duplicate of your friends in your contact list. You may save a comma-separated value (.csv) document of your friends to your phone and access it in Excel.

- Select File > Open & Export > Import/Export to open Outlook.

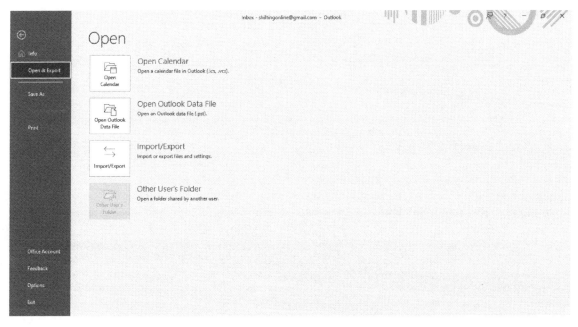

Figure 8: The Open & Export Feature

- Select Export to a folder > Proceeds in the Exports and Imports Wizard.

- Select Contacts as the file to download for your account after selecting Comma Separated Values on the Export to a File screen. Ensure the Contacts folder you select is linked to your e-mail address before continuing. This is crucial if you are executing these actions on someone else's PC.

- Go to where you wish to put the comma-separated values (.csv) file after selecting Next > Browse.

- After entering a file name, select OK > Next.

- To begin the export procedure, select Finish.

- Remember: Outlook does not provide a notification whenever the export procedure is finished.

Finding a contact from any Outlook module

You'd like to search for a person, but you're currently using another module. That's fine. Any Outlook module can be searched using the Search People box on the Home tab on the ribbon.

The steps are as follows:

- Find people by clicking on the "Seek People" box on the right of the "Home tab" of any Outlook module.

- Type the name of the contact.

- To open that contact's record in Outlook, press Enter.

- When you enter only a few letters of a name, Outlook lists names that contain those letters, so you can choose the contact you had in mind. For instance, with the word "Wash," you can search for Sam Washburn, George Washington, and any other people on your list that include "Wash."

- To view a contact record, double-click its name.

3 E-MAIL ORGANIZATION

3.1 Organizing Folders

By now, you are most likely used to arranging items into various folders. Windows helps to arrange all the other documents into unique folders. Outlook will also do the same. Create a folder and move your stuff into it.

Create a new e-mail folder

The simplest and most direct way to organize and manage emails is to archive them. Before filing a message, at least one folder wherein the file will be stored will be created. The folder is there for life unless you decide it is no longer needed, and delete it. After that, you can create as many folders as you need.

To create a folder, follow the steps below:

- Locate the Mail Module, choose the inbox option in the folder pane, or press the Ctrl + Shift + I buttons. If you were not doing some other thing before, the inbox should be selected by default when Outlook is opened.

- Choose the Folder tab and select the New Folder button on the ribbon. This will open the Create New Folder dialog box.

- In the Name text box, enter a name for the new folder. You can choose to use any name that suits you. You can also make as many folders as possible. There shouldn't be too many folders, either, to avoid confusion.

- Click on the OK button. The new folder will then be displayed in the Folder pane.

3.2 Move your messages to another folder

Filing messages can be as easy as moving them from their folder into another folder where you prefer them to be. All you need to do is open the box once they arrive and move each message to the desired folder. For another method of moving the messages to a different folder, follow the steps below:

- Locate the mail module > click on the message title that should be moved. The message will then be highlighted.

- Choose the Home tab option and click the Move button on the ribbon. The move drop-down menu will then be open.

- Choose the name of the preference folder to which the message should be moved.

3.3 Organize E-mails with Search Folders

You can sort your Outlook inbox and other folders using the search folders. The Search Folder offers one space where a specific type of message can always be found. A search will not move messages; it just creates a kind of imaginary section for messages. This way, you check through one message type at a time.

When MS Outlook is initially opened, there is no display of search folders in the folder pane. Therefore, if there is a need to use search folders, there will be a need to include one of the default search folders or make a search folder of your choice.

4 CALENDAR

On the other hand, the Microsoft Outlook calendar enables you to manage your work and home appointments simultaneously. So, it becomes beneficial if you frequently have work meetings at home. In addition, it helps in many ways, such as reminders, recurring appointments, and notes.

Outlook calendar lets you make a custom view of your calendar, which helps keep track of your appointments easily. Apart from this, the calendar allows you to add events from e-mails, which is more convenient. It also shows your most recent e-mail, phone calls, messages, and tasks. Moreover, it comes with new features that help you manage your schedules.

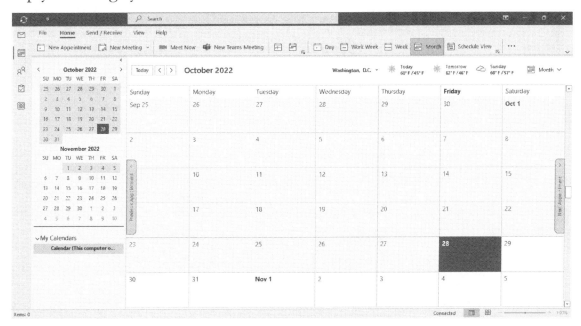

Figure 9: The Calendar Feature

The basic features of the Outlook calendar are highlighted below:

- Create an appointment on the go

- Manage appointments, meetings, tasks, and other items at the same time

- View your schedule at the same time as your team

- Share your calendar with your team

- Calculate a new appointment

- Create an event

- Create recurring appointments

- Calculate the due dates of your tasks

- Add comments to your events

Also, it allows you to share your e-mail with colleagues and clients. It also integrates with Windows, Mac OS, iOS, and Android platforms.

Moreover, you can edit your calendar directly in Microsoft Word and Google Sheets. Also, it has built-in integration with popular websites such as Google Drive, Facebook, Twitter, LinkedIn, Google Calendar, and others.

To start, open Microsoft Outlook and click on the "**Calendar**" tab. This will open up your calendar view, where you can see your upcoming events. If this is your first time using Outlook Calendar, it may be empty right now. To add an event, click on the "**New Event**" button in the top left corner of the calendar view. This will open up a new event window where you can enter all of the details for your event.

You'll first need to give your event a name and choose a date and time for it. You can also select which calendar this event should belong to (more on calendars later).

Next, you'll need to decide whether this is an all-day or half-day event by checking either the "**All Day**" or "**Half Day**" box next to "**Duration.**"

In addition to setting a date and time for your event, you can also set a reminder for it by clicking on the "**Reminder**" tab near the top of the window. Here, you can choose how far in advance before the start time of your event you would like Outlook Calendar to remind you about it.

You may also want to invite people other than yourself to attend your event. To do so, click on the "**Invite Attendees**" button at the bottom of the **New Event** window. A new window will pop up where you can type in the e-mail addresses of any attendees you would like to attend your event with you.

The first field in this window allows you to specify whether or not these individuals are required to attend; check off the "**Required**" box next to their name if needed. Then, once everything looks good, click "**Send.**"

Now that we've gone over adding basic information about an event let's discuss some advanced features available in Outlook Calendar. One such feature is recurrence; with recurrence enabled, you can manage your time by automating recurring tasks. For example, you can use recurrence to create appointments, reminders, and tasks that repeat at fixed intervals or on specific dates.

To create a recurring appointment, reminder, or task, open the relevant window in Outlook and click on the "**New**" button. In the resulting dialogue box, select "**Recurring**" from the list of options and specify how often you want the task to repeat. You can also choose to have Outlook remind you before each task occurrence.

Once you've created a recurring item, it will appear in your calendar or task list with an orange bar, indicating that it's scheduled for recurrence. To change any details about how often the item repeats or when it occurs, double-click on it and make your changes in the resulting dialogue box.

4.1 How To Insert Calendar To E-mail

There are a few ways to insert a calendar into an e-mail in Microsoft Outlook. To start, open the e-mail you want to send and click on the "**Insert**" tab. Then, select "**Calendar.**" This will open up a new window for choosing which calendar to insert.

If you have an appointment or meeting that you want to include in your e-mail, click on the time slot, and it will automatically be inserted into the body of your e-mail. You can also add text around it if desired. If there is more than one event happening at that time, Outlook will give you the option of which event to include in your message.

If you want to send someone a link to your calendar so they can view it online, go back to the "**Insert**" tab and select "**Link.**"

In the window that pops up, type in https://calendar.google (or whatever web address for your specific calendar) and hit **enter.** Your recipient will then be able to see and edit any events on your calendar.

4.2 How To Create an Appointment

Microsoft Outlook is a program that allows you to manage your e-mail, calendar, and contacts. You can create appointments from your e-mail by following these steps:

Step 1: Open Outlook and click on the Calendar tab.

Step 2: In the Calendar pane, click on **New Appointment**.

Step 3: The Appointment window will open. In the Subject field, type in a brief description of the appointment.

Step 4: In the Location field, type in where the appointment is taking place (if applicable).

If you want to invite people to attend this appointment

 Step 5: To invite people to attend this appointment:

i) Click on Add Attendees

ii) A list of all your contacts will appear

iii) Select which contacts you would like to invite

iv) Click OK

v) Repeat if necessary

vi) When finished adding attendees, click Close.

Step 6: Now we'll set up what time this appointment is happening:

i) Under Start Time, select AM or PM

ii) Use the drop-down menu next to End Time or enter a specific time manually

Iii) Click OK

iv). When setting up the date and time information for your new appt., click Close.

Step 7: Finally! Give your new appt some details

i) For the location, enter any pertinent info about where/when this meeting will take place

ii) For Description, give more details about what this meeting entails - be as specific as possible!

iii) If there are any attachments associated with this meeting (e-mail drafts or documents), attach them here

iv) Once everything looks good, hit Save & Close.

4.3 How To Create A Meeting

It's simple to set up a meeting in Microsoft Outlook. By selecting **"Meeting"** from the **"Create"** menu or by clicking the **"New Meeting"** button on the toolbar, you can create a meeting. When you create a meeting, Outlook will ask you for some information about the meeting.

The first thing you'll need to do is choose who will attend the meeting. To do this, click on the "**To**:" field and enter the names of all attendees. You can also type in e-mail addresses or names of groups if you want to invite everyone to a specific department or Office.

Next, you'll need to choose a date and time for your meeting. To do this, click on either of the two date fields and select a date from the calendar that pops up. Then, use one of the two-time fields to select an appropriate start time for your meeting. Finally, you'll need to give your meeting a name. This is optional, but it's helpful if you have multiple meetings with the same group of people. Once you've filled out all the information, click **OK** to create your meeting.

4.4 Microsoft Outlook: Share

Microsoft Outlook also includes features that allow users to collaborate with others by sharing calendars, contacts, and tasks.

To share your calendar in Microsoft Outlook:

Step 1: Open Microsoft Outlook

Step 2: Click on the "**Calendar**" tab

Step 3: In the "**My Calendars**" section on the left-hand side of the screen, right-click on the calendar you want to share and select "**Share Calendar**" from the menu that pops up.

Step 4: A new window will open, asking who you want to share your calendar with. You have three options: "**Public Folder,**" "**Specific People,**" or "**Groups**." Selecting one of these options will populate a list of people or groups you can share your calendar with below. If you choose either of the first two options, you'll need to provide at least one name for it to be shared successfully. For example, if you choose Groups, type the group name into the text box provided and hit enter/return on your keyboard). After selecting who you want to share your calendar with, click on the OK button at the bottom of the window.

Step 5: The window will close automatically after a few seconds, and your selected recipients will now have access to view (and optionally edit if permissions are granted accordingly) your shared calendar!

5 SECURITY

Microsoft Outlook has security measures that can be applied to prevent your e-mail from getting into the wrong hands. If you are receiving unwanted e-mails or links, these measures can help secure your e-mail account. Here are a few steps Outlook takes to protect your e-mail account: Save attachments to the hard drive before opening them. If you don't have an OLK folder, Outlook will create one. If you receive a message from an e-mail address you don't recognize, do not open it and don't click on any links.

5.1 What is a spam or junk folder?

To protect your account from unwanted messages, Microsoft Outlook Security includes the Junk E-mail Folder feature. These e-mails are sent when an account is modified or changed. You can turn this feature off or enable it depending on your needs. In addition, you can use filters in the Spam or Junk folder for additional security.

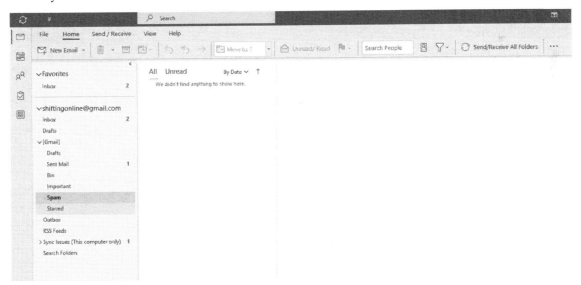

Figure 10: The Spam Folder

Junk e-mail messages are often classified as spam and are automatically placed in the junk folder. You can change this setting by checking the box next to No Automatic Filtering. However, higher protection levels may move legitimate messages to the junk folder. You can also set the Junk E-mail Filter to be more aggressive.

5.2 Filtering junk e-mail

The Junk E-mail Filter examines each new message received and determines, based on several criteria, whether or not the message might be considered spam. For example, both the time at which the message was sent and the contents of the message itself might be included in this category. The Junk E-mail Filter has its protection level set to Low by default and is switched on by default.

To set up the spam filter for Outlook.com, please do the following:

- Visit the **Settings** menu.

- Make sure that View all Outlook settings are selected.

- Go to the Mail menu.

- Choose the Junk e-mail option.

- In the column titled "Filters," check the box labeled "Block attachments, photos, and links from anybody who is not on my Safe senders and domains list."...

- Pick "**Save.**"

6 THE BEST OUTLOOK APPS/PLUGINS

Many users prefer using Outlook as their e-mail client and personal information manager. Over the years, as part of the Microsoft Office Suite, Outlook has proven to be a standard solution (in conjunction with the Microsoft Exchange Server) for both public and private organizations.

Even though without a doubt, Outlook is the option to beat, many freelancers and small companies cannot afford solutions intended for larger businesses. Still, there are lots of e-mail management programs aside from Outlook that can be used for free. Some of these are

6.1 Postbox

One-time Mozilla employees created this program, and hence was based on Thunderbird. About ten years later, the software has developed into an autonomous and extremely effective mail client. The design of its interface is like that of other solutions, and it is also easy to use. Users who want a unique look can adjust themes or design their templates.

For a more efficient operation, postbox makes use of different shortcuts. For example, users can access the Quick Bar via hotkey so that messages can be moved or categorized quickly. In addition, when creating an e-mail, a signature can be entered using the Quick Bar without the mouse.

There are lots of benefits when writing e-mails in the postbox. The software has various templates and text blocks that can be used to write cover letters and replies in a placeholder that can be added and created where the receiver's name is always added automatically.

6.2 Thunderbird

For both private users and those in companies, Thunderbird is one of the most preferred options as an alternative to Outlook. The open-source solution is also available for free. The program's free version is streamlined and offers only the most basic functions. One significant advantage is the addition of various add-ons. This means that there is room for expansion of the e-mail program. However, the add-ons and extensions are made to suit their respective versions. Therefore, if you need to update your version of Thunderbird, the add-ons must also be updated.

6.3 Spike

Spike was released in the year 2013, and it combines certain functions of classic e-mail programs with those that are used in modern messenger apps. For example, elements like subjects or signatures are no longer necessary immediately after a private mailbox is linked to the application. At the same time, the basic mail client functions, which include the central inbox or contact management, will be integrated into the modern messenger environment. It is also not coincidental that the creator of spike described it as a conversational e-mail application. Note that audio and video calls can also be made via the software.

The spike depends on modern standards in terms of security. For example, communications that include attached files can be encrypted with a single click. This way, you can be sure your messages are fully protected against unwanted access. Spike is free for private users; however, monthly fees are charged when business e-mail accounts are added.

6.4 Mailbird

Mailbird is an Outlook alternative that is only free in the test version. This e-mail solution combines messages and contacts from different accounts into just one box. The interface can be designed with different free themes as it best suits you. Mailbird offers different interfaces to various applications and also enhances the mailbox with helpful features for better interaction and teamwork. For instance,

Twitter, Whatsapp, Calendar, and Dropbox can be integrated into the mail to change it into a multi-functional program.

6.5 Integrating MS Outlook With Google and iCloud

Integrating MS Outlook with Google and iCloud is now possible. However, you need to take a couple of steps to make it happen. The first step is to paste the iCloud calendar link into Outlook. After you've pasted the link, Outlook will open its dedicated calendar feature. You can then choose between different options for importing your calendar. For example, to import your iCloud calendar, select the "from Internet" option and paste the URL into the appropriate box. Outlook will then sync your iCloud calendar with your Outlook account automatically.

6.6 Integrate Outlook with Google

Integrating MS Outlook with Google and I Cloud a great way to keep your calendar up-to-date on all your devices. You don't need to re-sync every time you make changes to your calendar; any changes you make are synced to all your devices. If you want to integrate iCloud Calendar information with Outlook, you can do it through the iCloud website

If you don't already have a Gmail account, you can set it up in Outlook for Windows. Then, you can synchronize your calendar and contacts with your phone via iCloud. You can also add your Gmail account to the Mail mobile app. Apple has a helpful guide for this process.

Integrating MS Outlook with Google and iClool is a great way to sync your calendars and other information across multiple platforms. In addition to keeping your calendars up-to-date across devices, you can also use iCloud to store and share data with others. Besides that, you can also integrate your contacts with HubSpot, a marketing e-mail tool.

If you're having issues integrating your calendars with iCloud, check if the calendars are being synced on your phone. If they're not, you'll need to stop the iCloud sync and restart Outlook. You can also try signing out and back into your iCloud account. If the problems persist, you can repair the Outlook application from Control Panel or the Programs and Features menu.

6.7 Integrate Outlook with iCloud

Integrating MS Outlook with Google and iCloud takes a few extra steps. First, you have to export your calendar from iCloud. This can be done through the iCloud app or the iCloud website. If you are using a Mac, you must first sign out of your iCloud account and then sign back in. This will allow you to sync your calendars, contacts, and e-mails.

iCloud works well with Microsoft Outlook. It supports the most recent versions of Outlook and Office 365 subscriptions. However, it's not a good fit for everyone, especially if you have POP3 e-mail accounts on multiple computers. Also, to use iCloud, you'll have to have a 64-bit version of iTunes, which is not included with Outlook.

To sync your calendar from iCloud to Outlook, you must log in to your Outlook account. First, click the Calendar tab and then click "From Internet." Next, paste in the URL of your iCloud calendar and press "Sync." Your iCloud calendar will now be synced with your Outlook account.

Integrating MS Outlook with Google and iCloud can be done in just a few steps. First, install the iCloud app on your computer. After installing the app, enter your Apple ID and password. You should then be able to check your e-mail and add appointments to your calendar. In addition, you can synchronize your contacts between Outlook and iCloud.

6.8 How to Integrate Microsoft Outlook With Your iPhone and iCloud

After downloading the Outlook app to your iPhone, you need to integrate it with your Google and iCloud accounts. Thankfully, there are several ways to do so. Here's a look at a few of them. Syncing iCloud calendar and contacts with Outlook is one such way. You can also sync your contacts and calendars from your iPhone with Outlook.

Syncing iCloud calendar with Outlook

To sync the iCloud calendar with Outlook, you must download the iCloud Control Panel from the Apple website. Once you have the panel, log into your Apple ID and password, and select "Mail, Contacts, Calendars and Tasks With Outlook." The data sync may take a few minutes, depending on your network speed. The new data will be applied to your iOS device the next time you open your calendar. You can also try to sign out of your iCloud account. This will stop syncing the iCloud calendar with Outlook, but you should still be able to access all your information. Once you're done logging out, sign in to iCloud again. This should resolve the problem.

Next, connect your iPhone to your PC via a USB cable. In the "Info" tab, select "Sync Calendars with Outlook." You can choose to sync all calendars or just the one you want to sync. After choosing a calendar, click "Apply" to begin the process of syncing. Note that you may have to disable iCloud while syncing the calendars.

Syncing calendars with iPhone

The first step in syncing calendars between an iPhone and Microsoft Outlook is to connect your iPhone to your computer. To do this, you must have the iTunes app installed on your computer. If your iPhone is not running the iTunes app, you must first turn off iCloud. Next, open the iPhone and connect it to your computer using the USB cable. After connecting your iPhone to your computer, the iTunes app should open automatically.

You can sync your iPhone with your Outlook calendar by connecting them to the same iCloud account. If you already have calendar events on your iPhone, you can choose to keep them on the iPhone. However, be aware that this may cause duplicate calendar entries on your iPhone. This is why it's essential to use a calendar backup tool, such as TouchCopy, which can copy all data on your iPhone to your PC. TouchCopy is free and can be downloaded from the TouchCopy website.

7 TIPS, TRICKS & FAQ WITH COMMON PROBLEMS AND SOLUTIONS

Ways to Resolve Microsoft Outlook Password Issues

Password issues are very common in Microsoft Outlook. Here are some reasons why you may be caught up in a password error loop:

- Outlook is not configured to remember passwords.

- The password for your e-mail address differs from the version Outlook has stored.

- Your Outlook login has become invalid.

- The program is broken and out-of-date.

- Outlook is unable to operate correctly because of security applications.

You may take several actions to prevent that and ensure that Outlook always remembers your password.

Method 1: When prompted for a password, click Cancel. This is the simplest solution that has, in some cases, been effective.

Method 2: Relaunch the laptop. Rebooting frequently resolves puzzling problems like this, so while it's not the fastest repair, it is one of the simpler ones to try. Restarting Outlook will enable you to reopen it from scratch and stop any potentially problematic background activities.

Method 3: By de-selecting, the 'Always' request for the login details box in the settings, you can force Outlook to store your login. If, after logging into the system, everything continues to function fine for a time, but later, you are prompted for it again, this is perhaps the most likely solution.

Method 4: Outlook's login for accessing your e-mail should be changed. If you change your login information but don't modify Outlook, the software asks for the username since it has no idea what it is. Also, if the e-mail address you're attempting to access requires two-factor verification, you may have to make a unique password only for Outlook.

Method 5: Access the 'Credential Manager' while Outlook is inactive, then clear out all the accounts related to Outlook/Office. First, select Windows Credentials, then click 'Remove' under the desired login details.

Method 6: While utilizing Outlook, log out from the Microsoft Office account you are currently registered with. This will not work for everyone because it could not be the identical e-mail experiencing the password problem. Sign out by selecting 'File'> 'Office Account.' After that, restart Outlook and sign in using that same interface.

Method 7: Install the most recent version of Outlook. Sometimes, a problem could be to blame, and the most updated version might fix it.

Method 8: Upgrade Windows if there are any newer versions. Some of these might have an impact on Outlook. After that, make sure to restart the laptop.

Method 9: Turn off all security features, such as antimalware software. If, after completing this, Outlook no longer requests the login information, you are aware that a privacy rule or program incompatibility is at issue and may check into it further. For instructions, go to how to turn off the Windows firewalls.

Method 10: Outlook should be launched in standby mode to stop add-ins from running. This is a bit of a stretch because all this procedure will establish the improbable scenario in which an add-in is at fault. However, if the login loop persists, it's simple to fix and will give you some guidance.

Method 11: Investigate a sluggish internet service. When you've been experiencing intermittent service, the login question can result from a lag in communication with the e-mail system. Again, moving nearer to the access point is the simplest approach to improve the Wi-Fi signal while utilizing a wireless connection.

Method 12: By selecting 'File' > 'Account Settings' > 'Manage Profiles' > 'Show Profiles' > 'Add,' you may create a new Outlook login. You may add the e-mail address again, presumably without the credential problem.

Method 13: Create a brand-new user account. Head To settings in Windows 10, for instance, and select 'Accounts' > 'Family & other users' > 'Add account.' Beginning afresh with a fresh user account has worked for some people to resolve the password reminder problem. Neither Outlook nor your existing user account will be deleted due to this.

Method 14: Activate Microsoft Support & Recovery Assistant (SaRA). This program does several tests to determine what might be incorrect with Microsoft Office and Outlook and, if feasible, will provide some fixes. When installing the application, select Outlook from the main menu, select Outlook, continue to ask for my login, and proceed according to the remainder of the on-screen instructions. This file is a ZIP format. After downloading the ZIP, extract its contents and launch SaraSetup to begin the setup procedure.

Method 15: Reinstall Outlook before attempting one more. There isn't much more that can be done to have Outlook recall your login now that a brand-new client account from the previous step and a brand-new Outlook setup has been created.

7.1 Threats to Avoid on Microsoft Outlook

Many people use Outlook as their main e-mail program. As a result, it poses a significant risk for malware, scams, and fraud. You may have read terrible stories of individuals forced to pay thousands of dollars to have their systems wiped out after becoming infected with malware, worms, and other terrible things. Unfortunately, both the threat and these tales are true. However, you may take a few simple steps to reduce susceptibility to such threats.

Here are some threats on Microsoft Outlook:

- ***Spoofing (sometimes called phishing)***: These e-mails seem authentic but contain fake links to other websites designed to fool you into divulging private information like credentials and banking information. Once they have your identification, the thieves can deplete your bank balances using this data.

- ***Viruses***: These downloadable files (also known as program files) can damage a drive or erase system files. Beware of files ending with ".exe."

- ***Bugs***: Without your understanding or cooperation, these software files or scripts utilize your internet to process bulk e-mails containing spam.

- ***Exploits***: These software files or scripts take advantage of security holes in your computer to send spam or carry out other malicious activities. These typically originate from obscure tools that certain websites have incorporated.

- ***Spyware***: These covert applications track your online activities (perhaps even the passwords you write) and send the information back to their creator.

- ***Adware***: These covert applications cause your browser to behave in a way that displays its adverts or pop-up advertisements on your screen.

- ***Inappropriate search taskbars***: These add-on toolbars substitute a company's sponsored search engine for your default search engine so that the outcomes of your queries display their promoted websites.

Such things threaten you. Now consider how to defeat them. Below are the top suggestions:

1. Windows Defender is the default antivirus application, but you may wish to upgrade to one with extra features and e-mail checking. Symantec (Norton) Antivirus, as well as McAfee VirusScan, are two widely used. Most comprehensive antivirus solutions provide e-mail screening for both incoming and outgoing

messages. Keep that function activated. You will be shielded against the majority of email-attached malicious programs.

2. Whenever you receive e-mails that have an attachment, be wary of it. Before you view the attachment, make sure the following:

- Is it coming from a familiar person?
- Were you hoping for a file from them?
- If the response to either inquiry is no, get in touch with the sender and ask what the e-mail is before you view it.

3. Always check any attachments that include the EXE, COM, BAT, or VBS data formats as an ending.

4. Be extremely wary if you receive a message with a ZIP-encoded attachment. (A ZIP file includes more resources.) One typical worm infection, for instance, disseminates itself via a ZIP file labeled as a digital greeting card.

5. Be extremely wary if you receive e-mail communication from your institution or a government organization. Most government and bank agencies avoid using e-mail for sensitive transactions. Instead, enter the web address into your internet browser to get straight there. Please refrain from clicking the message's link.

6. Be skeptical if you receive an e-mail from eBay or PayPal. These businesses occasionally do send out valid e-mails. However, phishing websites frequently pose as such websites. So avoid clicking the hyperlinks in the e-mails; instead, use your web browser to go straight to PayPal or eBay. It's more likely fraudulent if it doesn't address you by name in communication from PayPal or eBay. But this isn't a specific method to know.

7. Place the mouse cursor on links in e-mails that you're unsure about. The exact URL that the link points to is displayed in a ScreenTip. Again, it's likely a phony if it doesn't reflect the wording in the link.

8. Malicious search toolbars might deceive you into adding them to the program installation process. Typically, you may remove them via Windows' Control Panel.

(Right-click Start, select Control Panel and then select Uninstall an application under the Programs heading. Next, remove any installed apps that have "toolbar" in the name by scrolling throughout the menu of installed applications.

9. Yahoo! and Google toolbars are OK to maintain because they are authentic. Although they are optional, many individuals feel that any proprietary toolbar ruins the user experience of their browser.

8 ADMINISTRATOR OUTLOOK

To become a Microsoft Outlook Administrator, you must have basic knowledge of Outlook. There are many different ways to do this, including using the Outlook admin center. This article will help you navigate the admin center and configure Outlook. Once you know what to do, you will be well on becoming a Microsoft Outlook Administrator.

Knowledge to become an MS Outlook Administrator

MS Outlook is a popular e-mail program for many businesses. It can sort e-mails, locate colleagues, and set automatic replies when you're out of the Office. It can also manage your calendar to help you organize events. However, to become an effective administrator, you should know how to set up the software properly and learn how to customize it to meet your specific needs.

Outlook admin center

If you're having trouble accessing your e-mails, use Outlook on the web or the mobile client. The Outlook admin center is also where you can set the default signature for new e-mails.

Admins can set permission levels and assign end-user roles. These roles, which begin with the prefix My, enable administrators and specialist users to assign rights to end users. The admins can then control which settings end-users can access, change, or delete. The admins can also modify these policies by creating new ones.

9 THE STRATEGIC SHORTCUTS

SHORTCUT KEYS	FUNCTIONS
Ctrl + 1	Switch to the Mail app.
Ctrl + 2	Switch to the Calendar app.
Ctrl + 3	Switch to the Contact app.
Ctrl + 4	Switch to the Task app.
Ctrl+5	Switch to the Note app.
Ctrl+6	Switch to Inbox Folder.
Ctrl + Y	Go to the Folder dialog box.
Ctrl + Shift + B	Open your Contact Address book.
Ctrl + Shift + M	Open a new E-mail Message.
Ctrl +Shift + A	Open a new Calendar Appointment.

SHORTCUT KEYS	FUNCTIONS
Ctrl + Shift + Q	Open a new Meeting request.
Ctrl + Shift + C	Open a new Contact.
Ctrl + Shift + L	Open a new Contact group.
Ctrl + Shift + K	Open a new Task.
Ctrl + Shift + N	Open a new Note.
Alt + Q	Open a Search Box.
Ctrl + Alt + K	Search the current folder.
Ctrl + Alt + A	Search all the folders.
Ctrl + Shift + F	Open the Advanced Search.
Ctrl + R	Reply to a received e-mail message.

SHORTCUT KEYS	FUNCTIONS
Ctrl + Shift + R	Reply All to a received e-mail message.
Ctrl + F	Forward an e-mail message.
Ctrl + Alt+ F	Forward an e-mail as an attachment file.
Ctrl + U	Mark a received message as unread.
Ctrl + Q	Mark a received message as read.
Ctrl + Shift + G	Flag a message with a follow-up.
Ctrl + Alt + J	Mark a message as "not junk."

SHORTCUT KEYS	FUNCTIONS
Ctrl + Alt + 1	Show today's date.
Ctrl + Alt + 2	Show the current workweek.
Ctrl + Alt + 3	Show the current week.
Ctrl + Alt + 4	Show the current month.
Ctrl + P	Print an item.
F1	Help window.
Esc	Cancel a current task.
Ctrl + F1	Collapse or Expand the ribbon.

10 CONCLUSION

Microsoft Outlook 2022 is a powerful e-mail client with many features to help you manage your e-mail communications. In this user guide, we have introduced you to the basics of using Outlook 2022. Then, we have shown you how to create and send messages, manage your contacts, and schedule appointments. In this final chapter, we provided tips on making the most of Outlook 2022.

One of the great things about Outlook 2022 is that it can be customized to meet your specific needs. You can change the way it looks and behaves to match your preferences. For example, if you want more space in your inbox, you can adjust the settings so that messages are displayed in a list instead of in a column format. Or, if you prefer not to see images in e-mails, you can disable image loading for all or individual senders.

Another great thing about Outlook 2022 is its ability to integrate with other applications and services, such as Skype for Business or Microsoft Teams meetings. This allows seamless communication between co-workers or clients without having multiple applications open simultaneously. For example: While composing an e-mail message within Outlook, Right-click on the "To" field and Select "Add Participants" then, A window will appear with suggested participants from either skype/teams meeting roster OR contact list; from there, you can select one or more people from either list and Click "add" Message composition will now continue as normal, When ready click send as usual that's all.

In addition to integrating with other Microsoft Office applications such as Word or Excel, Outlook also offers a variety of tools that allow users greater control over their schedules and time commitments. These tools include; The ability to set up task reminders which will notify users via pop-up notification/sound alert /e-mail message when tasks are due, The ability to create OneNote notebooks explicitly related to tasks assigned within Outlook, and The ability to track time spent on various activities by recording start & finish times against each task And finally the calendar sharing between multiple people use when working collaboratively on projects involving multiple deadlines.

Printed in Great Britain
by Amazon

20897655R10027